From Cradle to Silence
A Daughter's Heartbeat of Love and Loss

From Cradle to Silence

A Daughter's Heartbeat of Love and Loss

Dr. Sonali Sahu

BLACK EAGLE BOOKS
Dublin, USA | Bhubaneswar, India

 Black Eagle Books
USA address:
7464 Wisdom Lane
Dublin, OH 43016

India address:
E/312, Trident Galaxy, Kalinga Nagar,
Bhubaneswar-751003, Odisha, India

E-mail: info@blackeaglebooks.org
Website: www.blackeaglebooks.org

First International Edition Published by
Black Eagle Books, 2025

FROM CRADLE TO SILENCE
A Daughter's Heartbeat of Love and Loss
by Dr. Sonali Sahu

Copyright © Dr. Sonali Sahu

All rights reserved. No part of this publication may be reproduced, stored in a retrieval system, or transmitted, in any form or by any means, electronic, mechanical, photocopying, recording or otherwise without the prior permission of the publisher.

Cover & Interior Design: Ezy's Publication

ISBN- 978-1-64560-749-6 (Paperback)

Printed in the United States of America

Dedicating this collection of my deepest emotions
To the hand that gave me life,
To my mother… my dearest Mummy,
Forever my heart, my guide, my soul.

The Voice I Carry

This collection of poems is a journey of love, loss, grief, and remembrance—a tribute to the most precious soul in my life, my mother. From my earliest childhood memories to the days of her illness, passing, and beyond, these poems capture moments both tender and painful, moments that shaped who I am.

Each poem is a conversation with her—sometimes a whisper, sometimes a cry. Through these verses, I remember her care, her sacrifices, her laughter, and her strength. I relive the moments she held me close, guided me through life, and protected our family. I also share the void left in her absence, the helplessness, and the unbearable pain of losing her.

Even in grief, there is a thread of hope—her presence continues to guide me, silently, invisibly. These poems are a testament to the eternal bond between a mother and her children. They speak of how love never truly leaves, how memory becomes a home, and how a mother's essence can live forever in her family, even after she is gone.

A mother is the first light of our lives. She is the

source of unconditional love, nurturing care, and wisdom that shapes us long before we can even understand the world. In her embrace, we find safety; in her eyes, we find guidance; in her voice, we find comfort. The presence of a mother is the foundation of every child's life. Yet, too often, we take her love for granted—assuming she will always be there. The truth, as these poems painfully remind me, is that a mother's presence is precious, fragile, and irreplaceable. Losing her is a wound that no passage of time can entirely heal.

Our ancient texts too remind us of the significance of a mother. The Atharva Veda says:

"Māto Devo Bhava"—"Treat your mother as God."

A mother is the embodiment of divinity in our lives, and her love is unparalleled. The Manusmriti emphasizes:

"Matru devo bhava, Pitru devo bhava"—"Honor your mother and father as divine beings."

These Shlokas remind us that parents, and especially mothers, are not merely caregivers but sacred beings who shape our existence. A mother carries the child for nine months, nurturing life within herself, often sacrificing her own comfort, health, and needs. Her love is selfless, unwavering, and eternal.

Through these poems, I also reflect on the subtle ways in which a mother's influence continues even after her physical presence fades. Her lessons, her care, her laughter, and even her silence guide us. She is present in our daily actions, our decisions, and in the love we extend to others. She becomes our moral compass, our silent mentor, and the voice that whispers strength when we are weakest.

These poems are not only my personal homage to my mother but a gentle reminder to every reader: never take your mother for granted. Life is unpredictable, and the moments we spend with her—whether teaching, scolding, laughing, or simply sitting together—are treasures beyond measure. Cherish her, honor her, and let her know she is loved every day, for once she is gone, no wealth or achievement can replace the warmth she gave us.

In these pages, you will find stories of childhood, small joys, care, illness, helplessness, and final separation. You will read about the days of COVID, when her strength shone even in adversity; the helplessness of hospitals and silence; the rituals and grief that followed her passing; and the continuing presence of her love in my life, my family, and my daughter. Every poem is a step through sorrow and a step toward remembrance, a way of keeping her alive in memory and in spirit.

My hope is that this book becomes a bridge—for me, for my family, and for every reader—between loss and love, grief and gratitude. It is a call to value our mothers while we can, to honor them, and to recognize that the lessons, love, and guidance they give us are among life's greatest gifts. They are the roots that sustain us, the wings that allow us to rise, and the light that guides us home, even when all seems dark.

This collection, therefore, is both a personal journey and a universal message: mothers are sacred, irreplaceable, and eternal in the hearts of their children. May these poems remind every reader of the blessing of a mother's love and the duty to cherish it.

- **Sonali Sahu**
(The princess of my mother)

Contents

My Beloved Mother	13
The Silent Warrior	14
Your Victory in My Steps	15
Walking Beside Me	16
The Taste of Your Love	17
My First Word, Maa	18
A Guest from Heaven	19
The Care That Bled Inside	20
Claps of Pride	21
Pain shared, Love multiplied	22
Heartbeat in the Yard	23
Wheels of Care	24
The Morning Thought	25
Guarded by Your Prayers	26
Guided Steps to College	27
Wings of Trust	28
Protected From Afar	29
A Mother's Wish	30
The Day You Let Me Go	31
A Fish Without Water	32
The First Homecoming	33
Everything, Yet Nothing	34
We Live in Each Other	35
You Made It Easy	36
Lessons of Balance	37
When Motherhood Knocked	38
The Taste of a Mother's Love	39
The Day of My Delivery	41

Circle of Love	42
You Lifted Me Again	43
Two Generations in Your Arms	44
How Do I Say Sorry ?	45
A Life for Me	46
Everything Repeats	47
Where Are You ?	48
When the Curse Came	49
The Day Silence Entered	50
Helpless Hours	52
That Afternoon	54
Her last breath, my first pain	56
When Silence Fell	58
Unbearable Goodbye	59
When You Returned, But Not to Stay	61
The Last Time I Dressed You	63
After the Fire	65
Twelve Days Without You	66
After You Left	67
The Empty Spaces You Left	69
Alone in the Crowd	71
Even from Heaven	72
Empty Celebrations	73
Your Presence Everywhere	74
Carrying Your Heart	75
Little Hands, Big Love	76
Where There Is Daughter	77
Returning to the River	78
The First Anniversary	79
The Terrace Between Us	80
Owing You	81
Signed in Life and Death	82

My Beloved Mother

You signed my birth certificate
With trembling hands,
yet long before ink touched paper,
you had already inscribed me
in the sacred scripture of your heart.

For nine months,
you carried not just my body,
but my destiny—
cradling me in the cradle of your prayers,
bearing pain with a silence only love knows.
And when I arrived,
the world blurred before your gaze—
your eyes poured pure light,
your arms became my first sanctuary,
my eternal refuge.

Maa—
you are the prologue to every chapter of me,
the quiet rhythm beneath my breath,
the hidden strength in my steps.
You are the reason
I met love before I even knew its name.

The Silent Warrior

I have watched you, Mother,
forsaking nights of rest,
rocking my fragile world with arms
that never tired of love.

I have seen you deny yourself—
a plate left untouched,
dark circles deepening,
yet your smile never fading.

Every sacrifice you wove in silence
became the foundation of my life.
You are not just my mother,
you are the strength behind my soul.

Your Victory in My Steps

The first time I stood on my wobbly legs,
you wept—not from sorrow,
but from the joy that spilled out of your soul.
I heard later how you called everyone,
your voice trembling with pride,
"Look! She is standing!"

You clapped as though the heavens had opened,
your eyes shining brighter than the morning sun.
That fragile step of mine
was to you a victory grander than any crown,
as if the whole world had bowed to your love.

Now I know, Mother—
every step I take, every height I reach,
was first your triumph,
your gift, your glory.
My life is nothing but the echo
of your unending sacrifice.

Walking Beside Me

I slowly took my first uncertain steps,
and you walked beside me,
mirroring every move.

You bent your stoop to meet my height,
lowered yourself to my tiny world,
so I would never feel alone.

I giggled with delight,
and in that laughter you found your universe—
as if you had received everything
life could ever give.

The Taste of Your Love

The first time you changed my diet,
from milk to rice,
I ate a little, then frowned—
my face twisted in dislike.

You laughed, yet worried too,
and ran to the kitchen in haste,
trying every recipe your heart could weave,
just to please my tiny tongue.

How much you did, Maa—
feeding me not just food,
but love, patience,
and the flavor of your endless care.

My First Word, Maa

I had just learned to hold the chalk,
my tiny fingers trembling on the earthen slate.
I scribbled in crooked lines,
lost in my childish attempts.

You held my hand so gently,
guiding each stroke with patience.
Together we wrote—
not just letters, but love.

And the first word I etched in life
was Maa—
the word that began my world,
the name that will never end.

A Guest from Heaven

My first birthday was never mine, Maa—
it was your grand celebration,
your festival of joy.

I heard how you ran like mad that day,
from room to room,
your heart dancing faster than your feet,
as though the whole world had arrived.

They told me you decorated me
like a divine guest from heaven,
wrapped me in love,
and crowned me with your prayers.

I was too little then,
but now I know, Maa—
my first breath, my first year,
was the holiest gift you ever received.

The Care That Bled Inside

My first day in school felt like your exam,
not mine.
Your hands trembled with restlessness
while I clung to you, crying not to go.

You smiled outside, but inside you bled,
your heart torn with every step away.
The whole day you were desperate,
hovering near the classroom walls,
watching me through a tiny hole in the door.

You whispered to my teachers,
"Please take care of her,"
as if entrusting them with your soul.
My mother, how much you cared—
more than words can ever hold.

Claps Of Pride

I stepped onto the stage for my annual day,
nervous, yet eager to shine.
But you, Maa, were already spreading the news,
as if I had won the World Cup.

Your joy in my small achievements
was greater than words could ever hold.
From the audience you clapped the loudest,
your pride echoing through the hall.

Leaning toward others with sparkling eyes,
you whispered with a trembling smile,
"See! That's my daughter."
And in that moment, Maa,
I understood what glory truly means.

Pain shared, Love multiplied

The days I fell sick,
you made sky and earth one in pain.
Your sorrow at my suffering
was far deeper than mine.

You soaked water in a cloth,
sponged me gently again and again,
measured my temperature with trembling hands,
never resting, never wearying.

My mother, how many nights
did the silent stars witness your vigil?
Your love burned brighter than any light,
carrying me through fever and fear.

Heartbeat in the Yard

I ran outside, chasing the sun,
laughing with new friends,
while you, Maa, were busy
in the endless swirl of household work.

Yet, again and again,
you returned to check on me,
each glance a sigh of relief,
as if I were beating gently in your heart.

Your love followed me in silence,
an invisible thread that never broke,
a presence that held me safe,
even in the midst of play.

Wheels of Care

My new cycle shone bright,
ready to carry me to school,
but you, Maa, stood firm with Father,
arguing, insisting I was too small, too fragile.

You wanted me strong, brave, fearless,
yet your heart trembled at every thought
that I might vanish in the crowd,
that the world might snatch me
 before your eyes could reach.

Time moved slowly as you watched,
your gaze tracing every passing moment,
until I returned safe and weary.
The food you kept warm,
 the hands that prepared it,
every act a silent pedal of love,
keeping me afloat in a world
you feared but never withheld.

The Morning Thought

Then your tension began, Maa,
what should go into my lunch box tomorrow?
Every night you planned,
thinking of the next morning,
making sure my uniforms were neat,
my bag and water bottle clean and fresh.

You wanted me to shine,
to face the world ready and strong.
After I returned, your question came—
"How was the food?"
Sometimes it irritated me, sometimes made me smile,
depending on my fleeting mood.

Yet you never wavered, never scolded,
never let my whims cloud your care.
You understood me perfectly:
My child must be tired,
this is just a temporary mood.

Guarded by Your Prayers

During my Board X exams,
your nights were sleepless,
coffee and glucose offered silently,
time after time, to keep me going.

I knew not then,
but you sat in the temple,
lighting lamps, chanting mantras,
sending prayers and good vibes my way.

Then came the day of results,
your hands trembling, your heart racing,
yet your face shone with pure joy
as you saw my accomplishments,
knowing every drop of your care
had guided me here.

Guided Steps to College

The day came, when I was to step into college—
that delicate, defining period of a girl's life.
You brought new bags, crisp clothes,
but beneath the surface of gifts lay your heart,
beating with hope, care, and caution.

You spoke softly yet firmly,
teaching me the life I should lead,
warning of distractions, fleeting temptations,
the trivial attractions of teenage years.
Your words were shields, your wisdom, armor.

And yet, you became my friend, my secret keeper,
the one I could share my fears and dreams with.
I carried your guidance gently,
woven into the very fabric of my being,
treading the world carefully,
anchored by your love and vigilance.

Wings of Trust

I stepped into the world of student politics,
a path filled with challenges and scrutiny.
Father was uneasy, worried,
but you, stood firm—
your faith unwavering.

"I trust my child," you said,
"Move ahead, explore, learn, conquer."
And with your words as wings, I soared,
facing every challenge with courage,
flying higher than I ever imagined.

I won, Maa—not just the contest,
but the victory of your trust,
the triumph of your belief in me,
the realization of the wings you gave.

Protected From Afar

With a heavy heart, you left me,
placing me in my grandparents' care,
as I began my university studies—
stepping into a world vast and unknown.

Every fifteen days, you sent Father,
your eyes searching, your heart restless,
and the phone rang endlessly,
carrying your voice across miles,
listening patiently as I poured out
my sorrows, my joys, my small victories,
my new lessons, my new friends.

Even from afar, your love wrapped me like a shield,
your words knitting safety around my heart.
I never longed for friends, never craved companions,
for your care filled every corner of my life—
you were my anchor, my refuge, my whole world,
my Maa, my universe,
guiding me through every step of my university journey.

A Mother's Wish

You sought the perfect partner for me,
one who could cradle my heart as tenderly as you.
But I whispered a different desire—
I longed for someone who would honor you,
the heartbeat of my life, my guiding light.

I found him,
a soul from distant shores,
tempered by struggle, carved by life's storms.
I, your princess, nurtured in love and warmth,
and he, imperfect yet steadfast,
ready to embrace the life we dreamed of together.

And you, did not falter.
You rose like a warrior of love,
fought through doubts, resistance, all obstacles,
to fulfill yet another wish of mine.
Your courage, your devotion, your boundless heart—
they are the invisible wings beneath every step I take.

The Day You Let Me Go

On the day of my marriage,
your hands were shivering,
yet you kept working, managing,
hiding the storm within your heart.

You smiled for the world,
but I knew you were bleeding inside.
How could you, my mother,
leave your own heart behind,
give away your soul to another home?

Every ritual was a quiet wound for you,
every blessing a tear you swallowed.
And yet, with trembling strength,
you placed my hand in his—
not because you were ready to let me go,
but because your love was brave enough
to endure the breaking.

A Fish Without Water

The neighbours whispered,
that after I left
you writhed like a fish pulled from water—
every breath a gasp,
every silence an ocean of ache.

They saw you weep inconsolably,
your voice breaking into sobs
that neither walls nor nights could contain.
You consoled Father with trembling words,
yet your own heart knew no rest,
beating itself against the cage of longing.

What they witnessed was grief—
what I know is love.
A mother severed from her child
is not merely restless—
she becomes a tide withdrawn,
an ocean waiting
for her lost shore.

The First Homecoming

After marriage,
I returned for the first time—
not alone, but with my soulmate.
The house was mine,
yet it felt strangely new,
as if walls had shifted
with my absence.

You welcomed me with warmth,
the kitchen alive with aromas
of every dish I once craved.
In your quiet way,
you slipped lessons between spices and laughter—
how to stir love into meals,
how to serve not just food
but affection and belonging.

You pressed into my hands
not recipes alone,
but your values, your essence,
your unbroken culture.
"Carry these with pride," you said,
"let them be your shield, your light,
your identity in another home.

Everything, Yet Nothing

The in-law's house was mine,
yet my eyes brimmed with tears.
Each minute stretched long,
woven with the ache of your absence.

I missed the lazy mornings,
where sleep lingered like a gift,
I missed Baba's gentle pampering,
the warmth of being a princess
in the palace of your love.

Here, I had everything—
a home, a family, a place to belong—
yet without you, without him,
all felt hollow,
as if the walls echoed only
the emptiness of what was lost.

We Live in Each Other

Never had I known the art of cooking,
yet you, shaped me from afar.
I called again and again,
and through the crackle of the phone
your voice became my recipe—
seasoned with patience,
stirred with love,
always gentle, never hurried.

I burnt my fingers once,
silent in my pain,
afraid to trouble you with worry.
But somehow, across distance,
you knew—
as if my hurt had echoed
inside your veins.

That day I understood,
the bond we share is not of bodies alone.
It is breath, it is heartbeat,
it is soul within soul.
We do not merely love—
we live in each other.

You Made It Easy

A new job,
my first steps into the world of work.
Professional life unfolded,
demanding, restless, unkind at times.
I shared every happening with you—
my irritations, my fatigue,
my struggles with the unknown.

Without you beside me,
each challenge felt heavier,
each day stretched endlessly.
I was learning, stumbling,
trying to find balance in the chaos,
yet it was never simple.

But you,
from afar, with words soft as balm,
with patience vast as the sky—
turned storms into passing clouds.
You made it easy,
carrying half my burden
without ever leaving your place.

Lessons of Balance

New challenges arrived,
new family members,
complications I had never known
stood before me like tall walls.

At times, I grew nervous,
my spirit trembling,
exhausted by battles
I did not know how to fight.
The world felt strange,
its ways unfamiliar,
and I—too new to belong.

But you,
from afar, still held my hand.
You steadied me,
taught me balance—
to bow down when love demanded humility,
to speak the truth when dignity asked for courage.
Through your wisdom,
I learnt that grace is strength,
and patience a deeper victory.

When Motherhood Knocked

The day arrived,
the one you had prayed for,
yet I stood unready,
shaken by the news:
I was with child.

You took my trembling hands in yours,
and with the wisdom of a thousand suns
you whispered what motherhood means—
a strength, a sacrifice,
a love that remakes the soul.

You were not just happy,
you were radiant—
your joy spilled into every corner.
You called Baba with tears in your eyes,
you hugged me so tight
as if holding two generations at once.
That day, you celebrated
not as the world celebrates,
but as only a mother can—
with heart, with soul,
with boundless light.

The Taste of a Mother's Love

Throughout my journey of motherhood,
my body wavered—
sickness weighed me down,
mood swings and irritations
clouded my days.
Health faltered,
and challenges stood like mountains.

Yet you stood unshaken.
You steadied me when I staggered,
balanced not only me,
but my home, my world.
You carried my burdens in silence,
reminding me always
that even as I was becoming a mother,
I would forever remain your child.

And then—
the pickles you prepared,
the recipes that danced upon my tongue,
the little care stitched into every flavour—
all were your ways of telling me
I was still your princess.
Every jar of spice,
every plate of food,

was love preserved,
your quiet devotion served warm.

You were strength in my weakness,
comfort in my restlessness,
and the eternal taste of home
in every stage of my life.

The Day of My Delivery

The day of my delivery,
you were more restless than I—
your eyes clouded,
your hands trembling,
your heart breaking
with every cry that escaped me.

The doctors whispered, "Have patience,"
but patience was never a mother's gift.
You consoled me with words soft as prayer,
yet inside, you were inconsolable,
bearing an invisible pain
no medicine could soothe.

And in those hours,
as waves of agony rose and fell,
I thought of you—
the pain you once bore for me,
the silent storms you endured.
That day,
I understood at last—
to be a mother
is not easy.
It is to carve love from suffering,
and strength from sacrifice.

Circle of Love

When my daughter arrived,
you were transformed—
from mother into grandmother,
your love unfolding
into a new blossom of tenderness.

You held her first—
your hands trembling,
your eyes raining tears of joy,
as if the heavens themselves
had descended into your arms.
In her tiny cry
you heard both a beginning and a memory,
my echo carried forward,
life repeating itself in gentler notes.

You called the family,
your voice a hymn of pride,
and the house burst into light.
Her arrival was honored
just as mine was long ago—
only now, I watched
as love completed its circle,
binding three generations
in one heartbeat of joy.

You Lifted Me Again

Then came the storms of married life,
obstacles I could not master,
burdens I could not bear.
I gave up,
I crumbled,
and fell into the dust of despair.

But you—
you lifted me once more,
raised me from my ashes
like a phoenix born of your faith.
My life was never the bed of roses
you had dreamt for me,
yet you never let me bleed upon thorns.

With every fall,
you laid your palm upon the ground,
so I might walk on your strength.
Here too, you arrived
with your timeless magic—
dispersing my pain,
scattering my agony,
until hope bloomed again
beneath my weary feet.

Two Generations in Your Arms

Night after night,
you became mother once again—
this time to your grandchild,
so I could close my weary eyes,
so I could breathe,
so I could rest.

You carried two generations in your lap—
first me, now her.
She melted into your embrace
as if she had always known
your heartbeat was home.
From your arms to mine
she learned what love means,
a lineage of tenderness unbroken.

You freed me from duties,
untied the knots of exhaustion,
so that I might fly,
chasing the dream I once whispered to you.
And as I soared,
I knew the wings were mine—
but the strength, always yours.

How Do I Say Sorry ?

Between profession, family, and child,
I was drowning.
Patience slipped through my fingers,
and the weight of the world
fell heavy on my heart.

I lashed out—
cruel, restless,
my words cutting where they should have caressed.
I turned my storms upon you,
the very shelter
that shielded me from life's tempests.

I know you were hurt,
your silence heavy with wounds unspoken.
Yet you endured—
understanding me more than I understood myself,
bearing the arrows
I should never have aimed at you.

Now I bleed within, Maa,
for every scar my lovelessness etched.
How can I gather the pieces of "sorry"
and lay them at your feet?
Words fall short,
but my soul kneels before you—
forgiveness is all I seek,
and your love,
the only cure I know.

A Life for Me

Not that it was ever easy for you, Maa.
Your body faltered—
BP rising like a storm to 220,
fevers burning through your nights.
Yet still, you ran for me,
ignoring your pain,
putting my world above your own.

You shifted your house near mine,
just to stay close,
just to be within a call, a breath, a step—
so I would never feel distance,
so I would never feel alone.

Every sacrifice you made
was silent, unseen.
Every expectation of mine
you carried like a vow.
Your whole life, Maa,
was not yours alone—
it was a sacred offering,
dedicated only to me.

Everything Repeats

You once woke early, Maa,
to pack my lunch box,
slipping love between layers of food,
watching me leave,
waiting by the door
for my return from school.

Now, time has circled back—
you do the same for my daughter.
Her little shoes, her ribbons, her books—
all touched by the same care
that once shaped my mornings.

Everything repeats, Maa.
The same patience,
the same warmth,
the same waiting heart.
My daughter is so fortunate—
for she is growing
in the very love
that raised me whole.

Where Are You ?

Your son-in-law and you,
wove a bond so rare, so tender.
I watched your eyes glow
whenever he was near—
shopping together for me,
standing side by side
at my daughter's PTM,
sharing laughter, sharing care.

You were his strength,
and he, yours.
Two souls, unspokenly tied,
protecting the world you both loved.

Now, without you,
he walks in silence—
broken, hollow,
his tears hidden,
yet I can hear them falling inside.
He too is searching,
asking the same question
that echoes in my chest:
Where are you?

When the Curse Came

Everything was flowing,
Life in its quiet rhythm,
Then the curse of COVID fell,
Darkening the skies of hope.

I faltered, I fell ill,
And you—unable to bear my pain—
Drew me close to your shelter,
Your home became my refuge.

Day and night you stood beside me,
Your hands carrying the weight of my weakness,
Your eyes whispering courage
When the world outside screamed despair.

Ambulance sirens haunted the air,
Roads lay empty,
Every corner echoed with loss—
Lives falling like fragile leaves.

Yet, amid the chaos,
Your patience became my medicine,
Your care, my breath of life.
In your arms, even fear bowed down,
And love conquered the storm.

The Day Silence Entered

Eventually you too fell sick,
Yet you kept moving,
Hiding your pain behind quiet strength,
No one saw it—
Until it became too heavy to bear.

That day, you were still feeding us,
Me and my little one,
Your hands steady,
Your heart trembling in silence.

Then—
A sudden suffocation,
A gasp that stole our breath away.
Worry spread like fire,
We rushed, helpless,
As they carried you to the hospital.

In those few moments of absence,
The house lost its heartbeat.
We could not manage,
Everything slipped into shadows.

You lay with oxygen by your side,
Fighting for air,

Each breath a battle,
Each moment stretching into eternity.

And at home,
Only silence lived—
A silence so deep
It swallowed us whole.

Helpless Hours

That day, I could not bear the pain,
My body too surrendered—
And I was carried to the hospital,
Needles and injections piercing through,
Restlessness flooding my veins.

At home,
My child sat all alone,
Eyes searching for comfort
In an empty room.
A helplessness too cruel to name.

The news reached you—
That I was admitted too.
Your heart, already fragile,
Broke a little more.
Your breaths grew heavier,
Your pain grew severe.

Baba stayed by your side,
But nothing could still the storm.
We were scattered souls in white walls,
Restless, breathless,
The rope of our family
Fraying, thread by thread.

Even today,
I shiver at the memory,
Those hours when time itself
Seemed to weep with us.

That Afternoon

The next day I returned from the hospital,
A little stronger,
Carrying the hope
That soon, you too would come home.

By afternoon, the call arrived—
You were searching for me,
Missing me,
Asking to see me at once.

Fragile, aching, masked,
I rushed to you.
And when you saw me,
You tried to sit—
Though breathless, sweating,
Your chest fighting for air,
Oxygen sinking to forty.

Still, your pride shone through the pain:
"See! She is my daughter—
My only daughter, my princess."

I had never seen you so miserable,
Yet never so radiant in love.
You laid your weary head on my lap,
My trembling hand resting on your forehead.

I begged, I pleaded—
Called for doctors,
Touched every foot,
Prayed for your breath to stay.

But they pulled my hand from yours,
Carrying you away to the ICU.
Even then, you comforted me:
"Don't worry, my child,
Nothing will happen.
I will come soon.
Chant the Mahamrityunjaya mantra—
All will be well."

And I returned home with empty arms,
While you remained,
In the silence of the ICU.

Her last breath, my first pain

From afternoon to evening
We sat in restlessness,
Hearts torn,
Eyes swollen with prayers and tears.

A pain we had never known
Sat heavy in the air.
Every breath was a prayer,
Every silence, a cry.

Then the call arrived—
Baba's hand trembled as he answered,
A voice from the other side,
Cold, final:
"Come and receive the body,
Your wife is no more."

That was all.
A few words,
Yet they broke our world.

Baba's face turned pale,
The color of sorrow too deep to name.
We stared at him—
Knowing the truth,
But unwilling to hear it.

He held me,
His eyes drowning in grief,
And whispered the unbearable:
"Your mother has left us."

In that moment,
Everything ended—
A silence sharper than death
Wrapped itself around our home.

When Silence Fell

All silence—
As if the earth itself
Stopped breathing with us.

Only the wall clock spoke,
Tick after tick,
The water tap dripping
Its cruel reminder of time.

Phones buzzed endlessly,
Voices calling,
But no one could cry.
Our throats locked,
Our hearts frozen.

We wanted to scream,
To tear the silence apart,
But grief held us captive.

Then suddenly—
A crowd gathered,
Near ones, dear ones,
Filling the gate,
Filling the air,
Yet unable to fill
The emptiness inside.

Unbearable Goodbye

All tried to console,
But their voices could not reach me.
I was deaf to comfort,
My hands still bound by the cannula,
My soul bound by loss.

I sat dumb,
Words lost in the flood of sorrow.

My daughter—
She had lost her world,
For she knew only your lap,
Your arms, your warmth.
Now she searched in vain.

My brother stood mute,
His silence heavier than tears.

And Baba—
His thirty years with you
Unraveled in a moment.
He wept without measure,
Crying inconsolably,
Calling out to the emptiness
That had stolen you away.

Your son-in-law was broken too,
Carrying a grief unspoken,
For in you he had found
Not just a mother,
But a shelter of love
Now gone forever.

When You Returned, But Not to Stay

Strange it felt—
Even from your silent soul
You balanced me,
Held me up through invisible strength.

I observed everything,
I grew,
I stood,
I walked outside,
Waiting for you to return.

Then the ambulance siren wailed,
Carrying you home.
Fear gripped me—
What would I see?
What could I bear?

Uff, the pain…
You lay sleeping silently,
Your face so still,
So far from the mother I knew.

I and your son
Stood frozen,
Our throats locked,

Unable to cry.
Only the broken words escaped—
"Mummy, Mummy…
Wake up, please wake up!"

But you broke your promise.
You told me you would come,
And you did—
But only to go again.

Your eyes stayed closed,
Your head tilted,
Blood trailing from your nose.
How much pain
Had you endured alone?

Had you searched for me
In those final breaths?
Called my name in silence
While I wasn't there beside you?

The thought haunts me still.
Every second,
I die again—
Wondering how your last moment
Would have been.

The Last Time I Dressed You

You dressed me my whole life,
Every occasion,
Every step,
Your hands shaping my world.

Now it was my turn—
To dress you,
Not for life,
But for your final journey.

A silk saree wrapped around you,
Sindoor placed gently on your forehead,
Alta painted on your beautiful feet.
How unbearable it was—
Only I know.

I did it,
My hands trembling,
My eyes drowning,
While everyone around watched silently.
They looked at me,
And I looked at you—
Miserably, helplessly.

Then the crowd moved,
To the graveyard,
To return you to ashes.

But even before the fire touched you,
I was burning already,
Burning inside,
Burning like hell.

After the Fire

My brother,
And your son-in-law,
Returned after hours
From your cremation—
Empty-handed,
Draped in white dhoti,
Faces pale with loss.

I was speechless.
No words to say,
Nothing left to do.
The house echoed
With unbearable silence.

For years to come,
We spoke to each other
Not with voices,
But through our eyes—
Heavy with tears,
Burdened with the same wound,
Carrying the same ache
That time could never erase.

Twelve Days Without You

All the rituals of twelve days
Were followed one by one,
Steps of tradition
Trying to guide our broken hearts.

Baba missed you terribly,
Yet kept himself busy—
Performing each ritual with trembling hands,
As though perfection could honor your love.

Food was prepared for you,
Carried to the terrace,
Placed with reverence,
Waiting for the crows to come and eat—
As our śāstra teaches,
A bridge between worlds.

We watched,
Silent, hollow,
Breathing but lifeless,
Simply existing—
Living without a soul.

After You Left

How we lived after that,
Only we know.
The world cannot imagine
The weight of our silence.

Relatives who once came often
When you were alive,
All changed—
Faces turned cold,
Hearts turned selfish.
No one asked,
"How are you living?
How is your world now?"

I saw those days—
Days without a mother,
And the world itself
Seemed selfish to me.

I became miserable, Mummy,
So miserable,
That even the mirror
Frightened me with my own reflection.

We ate not for joy,
Not for taste,
But simply to keep breathing,
To remain alive.

Life without you
Was not life at all—
Only survival
In an empty shell of days.

The Empty Spaces You Left

Baba forgets sometimes
That you are not here.
While watching TV
He calls your name—
Then the silence falls,
Heavy, unbearable.

We don't face each other.
I run to the terrace,
Or lock myself in the washroom to cry.
Then I wash my face,
Put powder on my cheeks,
So no one can see
The truth of my sorrow.
I pretend to smile again.

My daughter still chooses
The side of the bed
Where you once slept.
She talks to your photo
Every morning
Before leaving for school,
As if you are still listening.

And I, too,
Cannot pass by your chair
Without touching it softly,
As if your warmth lingers.
Each touch recalls your face,
Your smile—
Alive in memory,
Though gone from sight.

Alone in the Crowd

I feel alone in the crowd,
Even while riding to work,
Tears streaming silently,
Crying inconsolably,
Hiding behind black goggles
To mask my red, aching eyes.

At the workplace,
I remember your calls—
"Have you eaten? Are you alright?"
But now, there are no calls,
No gentle voice,
No shoulders to lean on.

I dial your number—
It still rings,
But no answer comes.
How deeply I miss you,
How can I ever say?
The world moves on,
But I remain
Lost in your absence.

Even from Heaven

So many obstacles came after you left,
Life no longer easy,
Every day a battle.

Yet, you were still there—
Though invisible,
Whispering from the universe.

Always, I found answers,
Strength to rise,
Confidence to handle the storms,
Guided by your unseen hands.

Even from heaven,
You never left me alone.
Your love became my anchor,
Your memory, my light,
Leading me through the darkest days.

Empty Celebrations

I don't celebrate my birthday,
For you are not here—
The one who brought me into this world,
The heart of every joy I knew.

Vacations feel hollow,
Echoing with absence,
Every celebration a reminder
Of the warmth I have lost.

Even laughter seems distant,
Even songs sound muted,
For every festivity
Now carries the weight of your absence.

Your Presence Everywhere

I open the cupboard,
Inhaling the scent of your sarees,
Seeking you in every fold,
Every thread a memory.

I touch your things,
Each one exactly as you left them,
The spices in the kitchen,
The little objects you arranged with care—
Everything remains,
Frozen in time,
Yet alive with you.

I feel your presence everywhere,
Every second,
In every corner,
In every breath I take.
Though unseen,
You are still here—
Guiding, watching, loving,
As if you never left.

Carrying Your Heart

Baba lost his everything,
All that he held dear
Faded when you left.
He is alone without you,
A quiet shadow of the man he was.

And I—
I carry your heart with me,
Trying to do the things you once did,
Trying to fill the space you left behind.
But how can anyone truly take your place?

He adjusts everything,
Eats less,
Manages more,
Silent in his sacrifice,
Trying not to burden me with grief.

Yet I see it all,
Every effort, every pause,
And I understand
The depth of love that lingers
Even in your absence.

Little Hands, Big Love

Now my little one tries to imitate you,
Wiping away my tears when I cry,
Whispering softly,
"Mumma, don't cry,
I am your little Mummy."

Baba tries to act like you,
Filling spaces you once held,
And your son, far abroad,
Carries a heart always heavy with longing.

I pretend to be strong,
But I am not, Mummy—
I believe you watch over me,
Guiding, protecting, loving.

Oh, how I wish I could touch you again,
Feel your warmth,
Hear your voice,
Even for a moment,
To remind me that
You are still here—
In little hands,
In quiet acts,
In every heartbeat of our home.

Where There Is Daughter

Where there is a daughter,
A mother never truly dies.

I carry your essence,
Your love, your strength, your soul—
Flowing in my every thought,
In every word I speak,
In every feeling I hold.

You live in me,
In the way I breathe,
In the way I love,
In the way I guide and nurture,
A presence eternal,
Unseen yet everywhere.

Through me, your heart beats,
Through me, your laughter lingers,
Through me, your spirit walks beside
Every step I take.

Though you have left this world,
You remain—
Forever mother, forever guiding,
Forever in me.

Returning to the River

After one year
When your asthi bisarjan came,
My brother carried you in an earthen pot
To the sacred Ganga.

That day, I felt myself die again,
As if you were leaving me once more,
Every step, every ripple of water
Echoed with pain,
Pain, pain, pain—
Surrounding me from every side.

The river received you,
Yet my heart could not,
For a part of me went with you,
Flowing into the currents,
Lost in the sacred waters,
Forever carrying your absence.

The First Anniversary

Your first death anniversary came,
People gathered,
Śrāddha was performed,
Voices, rituals, a crowd once again.

Yet I was still alone,
Standing quietly,
Looking at your photo,
Speechless at the journey—
From living you,
To this still image,
How can I ever explain?

Though others moved around,
Chanting and offering,
My heart remained in silence,
Trying to hold you,
Even in stillness,
Even in absence.

The Terrace Between Us

My house stands in front of yours,
The one you designed
So you could watch your only daughter every morning,
Our terraces facing each other,
Front to front,
A line of love built in brick and space.

But now, I am scared to open that door,
Afraid of the emptiness beyond.
I watch your home from mine,
Every window, every wall familiar…
Yet you are not there.

The space between us
Holds silence,
Holds absence,
Holds a longing that words cannot touch.

Owing You

Whatever I do,
I owe it all to you.

You never gave me the chance
To say I'm sorry
For my mistakes,
To hold you tight,
And release my heart.

You went away without a word,
Leaving a silence heavier than life itself.

My world is no longer bright,
No longer light.
It carries only weight,
A heaviness made of
Longing, regret,
And endless pain.

Signed in Life and Death

You signed my birth certificate,
And I signed your death certificate.
How cruel this fate is.

I read the paper thrice,
Where it is written
You are dead.

You left me with so many responsibilities,
And I am trying to bear them,
Believing you are still with me,
Listening, guarding, guiding.

I may not be the perfect mother you were,
But I am trying—
And I am sure
We will meet again,
In a world of heaven,
Once more.

Until that time,
Hold me tight,
Love me as you always did.

You were my heaven at your feet,
And my heart beats only for you.
I carry you,
And you carry me,
From wherever you are.

I miss you deeply,
And I will love you eternally.

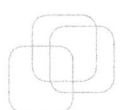

Black Eagle Books

www.blackeaglebooks.org
info@blackeaglebooks.org

Black Eagle Books, an independent publisher, was founded as a nonprofit organization in April, 2019. It is our mission to connect and engage the Indian diaspora and the world at large with the best of works of world literature published on a collaborative platform, with special emphasis on foregrounding Contemporary Classics and New Writing.